Lerner SPORTS

SPORTS TEAM SMACKDOWN

GOLDEN STATE WARRIORS VS. SAN ANTONIO SPURS

RIVAL RUMBLE

JOSH ANDERSON

Lerner Publications ◆ Minneapolis

To Adam: You're my favorite lifelong Spurs fan. I mean, Warriors fan. Oops!

The stats and information in this book are accurate through the 2024–2025 season.

Lerner Publications Company
An imprint of Lerner Publishing Group, Inc.
241 First Avenue North
Minneapolis, MN 55401 USA

For reading levels and more information, look up this title at www.lernerbooks.com.

Main body text set in Aptifer Sans LT Pro.
Typeface provided by Linotype AG.

Library of Congress Cataloging-in-Publication Data

Names: Anderson, Josh author
Title: Golden State Warriors vs. San Antonio Spurs : rival rumble / Josh Anderson.
Other titles: Golden State Warriors versus San Antonio Spurs
Description: Minneapolis : Lerner Publications, [2026] | Series: Lerner Sports. Sports team smackdown | Includes bibliographical references and index. | Audience: Ages 7–11 | Audience: Grades 2–3 | Summary: "The Golden State Warriors and San Antonio Spurs have one of the most storied rivalries in the NBA. Read about the top players, greatest moments, and key stats. Then, decide who wins!"—Provided by publisher.
Identifiers: LCCN 2025011455 (print) | LCCN 2025011456 (ebook) | ISBN 9798765689516 lib. bdg. | ISBN 9798348029371 pbk | ISBN 9798765699102 epub
Subjects: LCSH: Sports rivalries—United States—History—Juvenile literature | Golden State Warriors (Basketball team)—Statistics—Juvenile literature | San Antonio Spurs (Basketball team)—Statistics—Juvenile literature | National Basketball Association—History—Juvenile literature | Basketball—United States—History—Juvenile literature | LCGFT: Statistics
Classification: LCC GV583 .A685 2026 (print) | LCC GV583 (ebook) | DDC 796.323/6409764351—dc23/eng/20250606

LC record available at https://lccn.loc.gov/2025011455
LC ebook record available at https://lccn.loc.gov/2025011456

Manufactured in the United States of America
1 – CG – 12/15/25

TABLE OF CONTENTS

INTRODUCTION

GRASPING THE TORCH

Game 1 of the 2013 NBA playoff series between the San Antonio Spurs and Golden State Warriors was a classic. With 20 seconds remaining, Spurs forward Danny Green hit a three-pointer to tie it 106–106. The game went to overtime.

With time running out, Warriors guard Jarrett Jack drove to the hoop and hit a tough layup to tie the game 115–115. Spurs guard Manu Ginóbili had a chance to win at the buzzer, but his shot missed and the game went to double overtime.

Jarrett Jack shoots over two Spurs defenders during the 2013 NBA playoffs.

With the Spurs ahead 126–123 in the final minute of double overtime, Golden State star Steph Curry drove to the hoop. Curry passed to Kent Bazemore under the basket. Bazemore hit a layup that put the Warriors ahead 127–126 with just over three seconds left.

With one last chance, San Antonio forward Kawhi Leonard passed to Ginóbili behind the three-point line. A defender raced toward Ginóbili. He jumped and nailed the shot. The crowd erupted. The Spurs had won 129–127.

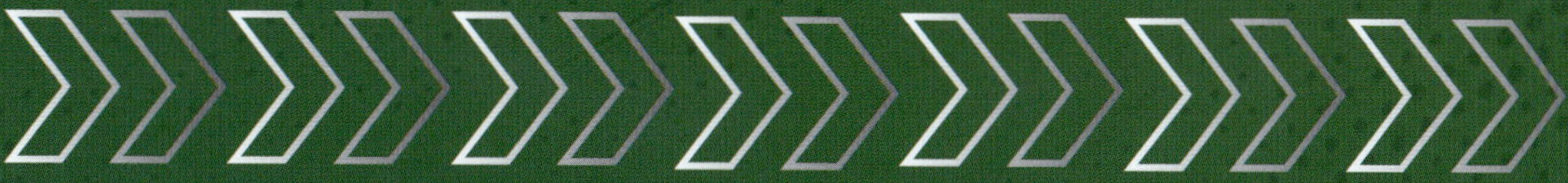

FAST FACTS

- At first, the Warriors played in Philadelphia.
- The Spurs won five championships between 1999 and 2014.
- From 2015 to 2022, the Warriors won four NBA titles.
- In 2023, the Spurs picked French center Victor Wembanyama in the NBA Draft.

San Antonio went on to the NBA Finals that year but lost to the Miami Heat. They won the last championship of their most dominant era the following season. Meanwhile, the Warriors were just beginning their NBA dynasty. They would go on to win four titles in eight years. The Spurs and Warriors have been two of the greatest NBA teams of all time. But which one is best? Let the smackdown begin!

David Robinson celebrates after winning the 2003 NBA Finals.

PAUL
3
SAN ANTONIO
1

SMACKDOWN!

GOLDEN STATE
23
WARRIORS
GOLDEN STATE
4
WARRIORS

CHAPTER 1

Standing just over 7 feet (2.1 m) tall, Wilt Chamberlain is considered one of the greatest NBA players of all time.

WESTERN CONFERENCE RIVALS

The Warriors began play in 1946 in Philadelphia as one of the first pro basketball teams in the United States. They won a championship in their first season and another in 1956. From 1960 to 1965, the team was home to the league's greatest player, Wilt Chamberlain.

Though the Warriors often made the playoffs during this time, they did not win a title. In 1962, the team moved to San Francisco. They moved across the bay to Oakland in 1971 and became the Golden State Warriors.

In 1975, star Rick Barry led the Warriors to their first title since the team left Philadelphia. They swept the Washington Bullets in four games in the NBA Finals. Another exciting period came in the late 1980s and early 1990s. Chris Mullin and Tim Hardaway led the team to the playoffs in five of eight seasons.

The greatest era in Warriors history began when they drafted Steph Curry in 2009. His three-point shooting changed the way modern basketball is played. Players across the league attempt many more three-pointers after seeing his success. Under Coach Steve Kerr, Curry and star teammates Klay Thompson and Draymond Green won four NBA titles between 2015 and 2022.

Steph Curry is considered one of the greatest shooters in NBA history.

The San Antonio Spurs were originally the Dallas Chaparrals. They were part of the American Basketball Association (ABA). When the ABA and NBA merged in 1976, the Spurs joined the NBA.

The Spurs made the playoffs in 47 of their first 58 seasons but didn't win a title until 1999. That year, Coach Gregg Popovich paired legend David Robinson with rising star Tim Duncan. The 7 foot 1 (2.2 m) center Robinson and 6 foot 11 (2.1 m) forward Duncan led the Spurs to victory in the 1999 NBA Finals. The pair won another title in 2003 before Robinson retired.

Before they became the Spurs, the team played in Dallas for six seasons.

Both David Robinson (left) and Tim Duncan (right) played their whole careers for the Spurs. They scored a combined 47,286 points.

Duncan and the Spurs won two more titles in 2005 and 2007, this time with rising stars Tony Parker and Manu Ginóbili. They won again in 2014, just before Duncan retired. That year, they were led by dynamic forward Kawhi Leonard. Popovich and Duncan's Spurs won five NBA titles from 1999 to 2014.

Tony Parker (center) and the Spurs lift the 2014 NBA Finals trophy.

French center Victor Wembanyama (right) shakes hands with NBA commissioner Adam Silver at the 2023 NBA Draft.

The Warriors surprised many fans by winning the title in 2022. Now, the Warriors hope to win their eighth championship before franchise icon Steph Curry retires. Meanwhile, the Spurs didn't make the playoffs from 2020 to 2024. Their luck changed in 2023 when they drafted French center Victor Wembanyama. He is already one of the league's top defenders and should be a future NBA superstar.

CHECK IT OUT

Spurs coach Gregg Popovich holds an NBA record with 1,412 regular-season coaching victories since taking over the Spurs in 1996.

CHAPTER 2

Wilt Chamberlain shoots over a New York Knicks defender in a 1962 game.

AMAZING MOMENTS

During the 1961–1962 NBA season, Warriors center Wilt Chamberlain set a record that still stands. On March 2, 1962, Chamberlain scored 100 points in a game against the New York Knicks. He led the Warriors to a 169–147 victory.

In 1975, Golden State faced the Washington Bullets in the NBA Finals. The Warriors won the first three games of the series. In Game 4, the Warriors trailed by 14 points early but didn't give up. A late layup by guard Butch Beard put them ahead 94–93. Then, Beard's free throws sealed a 96–95 victory. The win gave the Warriors their first title since 1956.

Game 5 of the 2005 NBA Finals between the Spurs and the Detroit Pistons was thrilling. The score was tied 18 times. In overtime, the Pistons led 95–93 with seconds remaining. Detroit's Chauncey Billups missed a layup to give the Spurs one last chance. Robert Horry gave the ball to Manu Ginóbili, who had two players defending him. Ginóbili passed back to Horry. Horry sank a three-pointer for a 96–95 victory. The Spurs went on to win the series in seven games.

Robert Horry (center) scored 214 points and had 125 rebounds during the 2005 NBA playoffs.

Steph Curry* (left) *and Klay Thompson* (right) *scored more than 600 three-pointers during the 2022–2023 season.

Steph Curry and Klay Thompson were called the "Splash Brothers" for their great three-point shooting. In 2016, Curry set a single-season record with 402 three-pointers made. He hit a record 13 threes in one game. Thompson broke his teammate's record by hitting 14 threes in a 2018 game. In the 2022–2023 season, the Warriors set an NBA team record with 1,363 three-pointers made.

CHECK IT OUT

Warriors forward Draymond Green has been selected to the NBA's All-Defensive Team eight times.

The Warriors missed the playoffs in 2020 and 2021. Many believed Kerr and the Splash Brothers were done winning titles. However, they returned to the NBA Finals in 2022. After losing Games 1 and 3 to the Boston Celtics, the Warriors took control. In Game 6, Curry scored 34 points. The Warriors won 103–90, and Curry was named Finals MVP (Most Valuable Player).

Curry (center) avoids two Boston Celtics players during a 2022 game.

David Robinson (left) led the NBA in rebounds twice. He grabbed 10,497 total rebounds during his career.

Spurs legends David Robinson and Tim Duncan have a lot in common. Both stand around 7 feet (2.1 m) tall and were known for their defense. The Spurs picked Robinson first overall in the 1987 NBA Draft, and Duncan first in 1997.

In 2023, after a challenging season, the Spurs got the first pick again. They selected Victor Wembanyama, a 7 foot 3 (2.2 m) center who is strong on offense and defense. Wembanyama hopes to follow in Robinson and Duncan's footsteps and lead the Spurs to future NBA titles.

Victor Wembanyama is one of only 12 current NBA players who are over 7 feet (2.1 m) tall.

CHAPTER 3

More than 3,500 of Rick Barry's 16,447 points for the Warriors came from free throws.

TOP PLAYERS

Hall of Fame player Rick Barry played for the Warriors in the 1960s and 1970s. He led the NBA in scoring during the 1966–1967 season with an average of 35.6 points per game. Barry led the league in free throw percentage seven times. He ranks eighth all-time in career free throw percentage.

Spurs legend David Robinson was known as the Admiral due to his college career in the US Naval Academy. He was a 10-time All-Star and eight-time All-Defensive Team member. In 1995, he became the first Spurs player in team history to win the league MVP award. Robinson helped lead the Spurs to two NBA titles. He is a member of the Hall of Fame.

David Robinson (left) led the NBA in rebounds and blocks in multiple seasons.

Tim Duncan (left) avoids a Warriors defender during a 2016 game.

Robinson's teammate, Tim Duncan, earned two NBA MVP awards and three Finals MVPs. A 15-time All-Star and 15-time All-Defensive Team member, Duncan led the Spurs to five NBA titles. After retiring, he joined Robinson in the Hall of Fame.

Steph Curry, a two-time NBA MVP and one-time Finals MVP, has guided the Warriors to four NBA titles. An 11-time All-Star and two-time scoring champion, Curry holds the record for most career three-pointers with 4,058 and counting. He also holds the record for the highest free throw percentage in NBA history with 91.1.

Steph Curry smiles after hitting a three-pointer during a 2025 game.

CHECK IT OUT

The Warriors set an NBA record in 2015–2016 when they finished with 73 wins on the season.

Draymond Green joined Curry on the Warriors in 2012. Known for his defense, he led the league in steals per game during the 2016–2017 season. Averaging 8.7 points, 6.9 rebounds, and 5.6 assists per game for his career, Green is a four-time All-Star.

Draymond Green dribbles down the court during a 2024 game against the New Orleans Pelicans.

Victor Wembanyama also plays for the French national basketball team. He won a silver medal at the 2024 Olympics.

Victor Wembanyama, the Spurs' young center, joined the league in 2023. He has been even better than expected. Averaging more than 22 points and 10 rebounds per game, he led the league in blocks per game in his first two seasons. "Wemby" won the NBA Rookie of the Year award in 2024. He earned his first All-Star selection in 2025.

CHAPTER 4

Players from the Warriors and Spurs battle for the tip-off during a 2021 game.

CHOOSE YOUR CHAMPION

Now that we've learned more about the Spurs and the Warriors, which team comes out on top? There's no such thing as a right or wrong answer. Different people will have different opinions.

The Spurs have appeared in the playoffs 47 times in 58 seasons. The Warriors have made the playoffs 38 times in 79 seasons. The Spurs have made the Finals six times and won them five times. The Warriors have only played in the Finals 12 times, and they've won seven championships.

The Spurs and Warriors get ready to face off during the 2017 playoffs.

The teams have matched up in the regular season 189 times. The Spurs have won 117 times. The Warriors have won 72. The teams have faced off in four playoff series, with the Warriors winning three.

This smackdown between two of the Western Conference's top teams comes down to one small edge. During their greatest era, the Warriors won four titles between 2015 and 2022. This eight-year period is one of the most successful in NBA history.

But the Spurs kept their place as one of the NBA's top teams for nearly two decades. They won five titles between 1999 and 2014. This amazing run of success gives the Spurs the very slight victory over their Golden State rivals in this incredibly close smackdown.

What do you think? Did we get it right? Think about why or why not!

SMACKDOWN TIMELINE

SAN ANTONIO SPURS

1973 The team moves from Dallas to San Antonio and changes its name to the Spurs.

1987 The Spurs select David Robinson as the first pick in the NBA Draft.

1997 The Spurs get the first overall draft pick again and choose Tim Duncan.

1999 San Antonio captures its first NBA Championship, defeating the New York Knicks in the Finals.

2003 The Spurs win their second NBA title, with Tim Duncan earning Finals MVP honors.

2014 San Antonio wins its fifth NBA title, defeating the Miami Heat in a five-game Finals series.

2023 The Spurs select Victor Wembanyama with the first pick in the NBA Draft.

2024 Wembanyama delivers a historic triple-double performance, scoring 34 points, grabbing 14 rebounds, and providing 11 assists, leading the Spurs to a comeback win against the Sacramento Kings.

GOLDEN STATE WARRIORS

1946 The team begins play in Philadelphia, becoming an original member of the Basketball Association of America (BAA).

1947 The Warriors win the first BAA championship and earn the first title in team history.

1962 The Warriors move to San Francisco, California.

1971 After moving to Oakland, California, the team becomes the Golden State Warriors.

1975 Led by Rick Barry, the Warriors win their third championship by defeating the Washington Bullets in the NBA Finals.

2015 After 40 years without a title, head coach Steve Kerr and superstar Steph Curry lead the team to victory in the NBA Finals against the Cleveland Cavaliers.

2016 The team sets an NBA record with a 73–9 regular-season record but falls to the Cavaliers in a seven-game Finals series.

2022 The Warriors win their seventh NBA championship, defeating the Boston Celtics in the Finals.

GLOSSARY

All-Star: a player chosen as one of the best in the league to compete in a game against other top players

assist: a pass that leads directly to a basket

draft: when teams take turns picking new players

Hall of Fame: a museum in Springfield, Illinois, that honors the best players in basketball history

layup: a shot in basketball made from near the basket usually by playing the ball off the backboard

NBA Finals: a series of games to decide each year's NBA champion

overtime: extra time added to a game when the score is tied at the end of normal playing time

playoffs: a series of games played to decide a champion

rival: a team or player who tries to be more successful than another

swept: when a team wins a series without losing any gamess

LEARN MORE

Britannica Kids: Stephen Curry
https://kids.britannica.com/students/article/Stephen-Curry/629891

Britannica: Victor Wembanyama
https://www.britannica.com/biography/Victor-Wembanyama

Ducksters: NBA
https://www.ducksters.com/sports/national_basketball_association.php

Flynn, Brendan. *The NBA Encyclopedia for Kids*. ABDO, 2022.

Stabler, David. *Inside the Golden State Warriors*. Lerner Publications, 2023.

Stewart, Mark. *The San Antonio Spurs*. Norwood House Press, 2025.

INDEX

PHOTO ACKNOWLEDGMENTS

Image credits: Ronald Martinez/Getty Images, p. 4; Jed Jacobsohn/Getty Images, p. 6; Ronald Cortes/Getty Images; Thearon W. Henderson/Getty images, p. 7; James Drake/Getty Images, p. 8; Jed Jabosohn/Getty Images, p. 9; Bettmann/Getty Images, p. 10; PAUL BUCK/AFP/Getty Images, p. 11; Andy Lyons/Getty Images, p. 12; Sarah Stier/Getty Images, p. 13; Bettmann/Getty Images, p. 14; Brian Bahr/Getty Images, p. 15; Ray Chavez/MediaNews Group/The Mercury News via Getty Images/Getty Images, p. 16; San Francisco Chronicle/Hearst Newspapers/Getty Images, p. 17; Ronald Martinez/Getty Images, p. 18; G Fiume/Getty Images, p. 19; Bettmann/Getty Images, p. 20; Focus on Sport/Getty Images, p. 21; Nhat V. Meyer/MediaNews Group/Bay Area News via Getty Images/Getty Images, p. 22; Thearon W. Henderson/Getty Images, p. 23; Kevin Mistry/Getty Images, p. 24; Ronald Cortes/Getty Images, p. 25; Thearon W. Henderson/Getty Images, p. 26; Jose Carlos Fajardo/MediaNews Group/Bay Area News via Getty Images/Getty Images, p. 27.

Cover: Melissa Tamez/Icon Sportswire/Newscom; Melissa Tamez/Icon Sportswire/Newscom; Melissa Tamez/Icon Sportswire/Newscom.